To those who take the time
to fly-fish with a child.

You have untangled lines
and tied on flies,
time and time again.

You have passed on
respect and responsibility,
history and traditions.

Thank you!

Fly-Fishing with Trout-tail

A Child's Journey

I am Trout-Tail.
I love to fly-fish!

Do you know that
Fly-fishing is
more,
much more,
than catching fish?
Come with me and you'll see!

Fly-fishing is ...

magical places

with water and trees and rocks to climb on.

Fly-fishing is ...

Clothes and
gear and
gadgets
hanging from your vest!

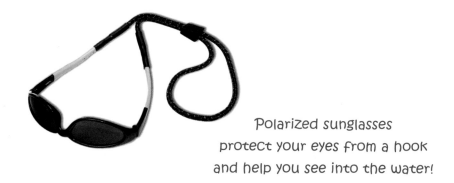

Polarized sunglasses
protect your eyes from a hook
and help you see into the water!

release net

fly rod and reel

hip waders

pack basket

hat with visor

fly box

vest

Fly-fishing is ...

loving nature.

My family always says:

Leave it better than you found it!

Fly-fishing is ...

different from bait fishing.

spin reel and rod

Spin casting line is thin and light.
You use worms and fish as bait.

FLY FLY FLY FLY

Fly-fishing line is **thick** and heavy.
You use a man-made fly (not live bait).
The line is the weight that lets you cast the fly.

fly reel and rod

Fly-fishing is ...

about the flies!

Flies can be flashy with bright colors!

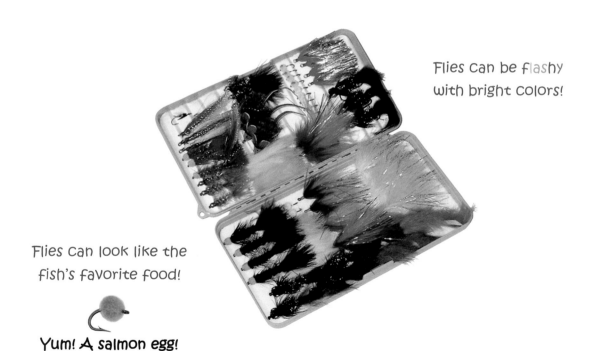

Flies can look like the fish's favorite food!

Yum! A salmon egg!

This is a Green Butt fly.  A fly is made on a hook.

(my favorite!)

Here is my fly box,
filled with lucky flies!

Fly-fishing is ...
art!

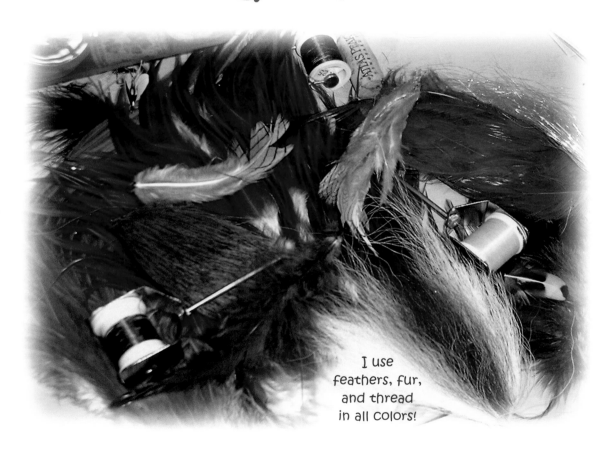

I use feathers, fur, and thread in all colors!

Fly-fishing is ...

learning to do it yourself.

I can tie on my own fly!

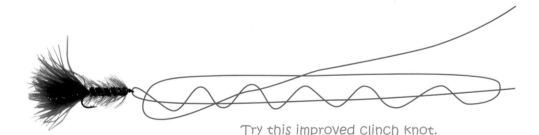

Try this improved clinch knot.

Fly-fishing is ...

new words,
silly words,
fun words!

The nippers clip the tippet off the Green-butt skunk!

Green-butt skunk!

Tippet
ties the fly to the leader.

Nippers
are sharp edged clippers.

There was a fish,
the most beautiful fish
that you ever did see...

and the reel on the rod and the rod in the hand of the child who's fishing

and the tippet on the leader and the leader on the line

backing on the reel and the tippet and the backing and the line on the fly on the tippet

There's a fish on the fly

in the clear
cold river at dawn!

Fly-fishing is ...

getting the fly to the fish!

You don't need a big, beautiful cast!
Look for spots where a

"flick and d'oink"

of the rod
will land the fly where it needs to be!

Keep it simple, with a little bit of line!

Fly-fishing is ...

feeling **proud**,
even if the catch is small!

I found the hole.
I saw the fish. I picked out my fly.

I flicked my fly out over the fish and "WHAM"!
He thought my egg sucking leech looked good enough to eat!

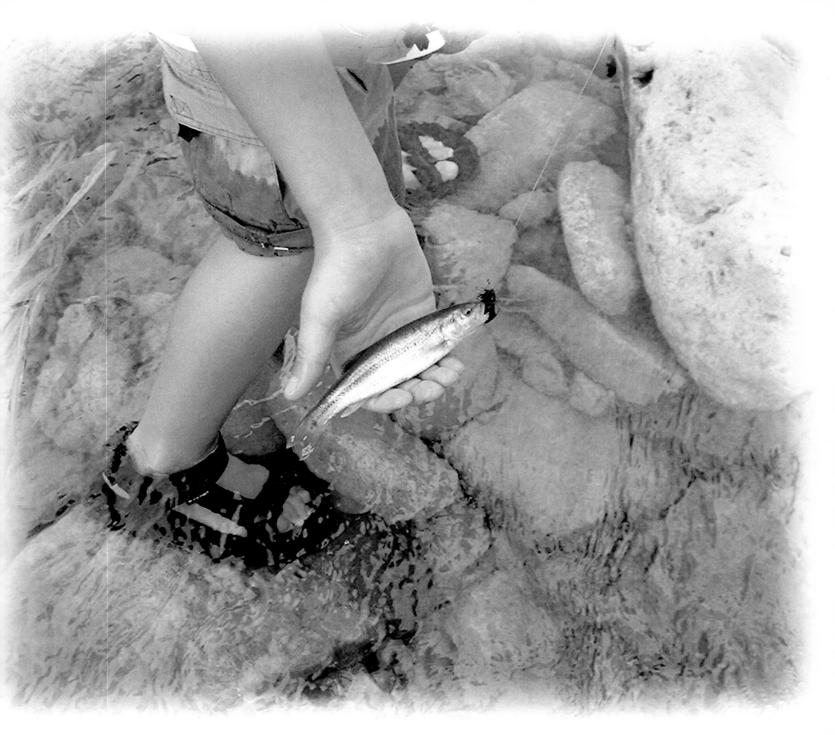

Fly-fishing is ...

releasing it back to the water,
alive and happy!

Keep it wet and unhook it gently.
This little guy deserves to get bigger!

Fly-fishing is ...

finding your own

secret

hot

spot!

Fly-fishing is ...

the surprises you find
at the river!

Whisper

Stay quiet so this
baby moose won't
be scared!

Fly-fishing is ...

being together.

And remember,

Fly-fishing is ...

sometimes

about

Catching fish!

Glossary

Tippet   Connects the fly to the leader. It is very thin, clear and almost invisi[ble]

Leader   Connects the tippet to the fly line. It is thin and clear.

Line   Provides the weight and length for the cast. It is thick, heavy and colored.

Backing   Connects the fly line to the reel.
Adds length to the fly line and thickness
to the reel so the line won't get loopy kinks.

Reel   Stores the backing and line. It attaches to the rod.

Polarized sunglasses   The 'polarized' coating cuts down the glare from the sun
and lets you see into the water.

Tail-Notes

1. Did you notice that there is a fly on almost every page?
Some are hidden. Some are not. Can you find them all?

2. Learn the names of the flies from the back of the book.
Now try to name the flies on each page!

Send your fly-fishing stories and pictures to me! trouttail@trouttail.com

I hope you had fun!

Remember: It's OK to say Green Butt when you're fly-fishing!

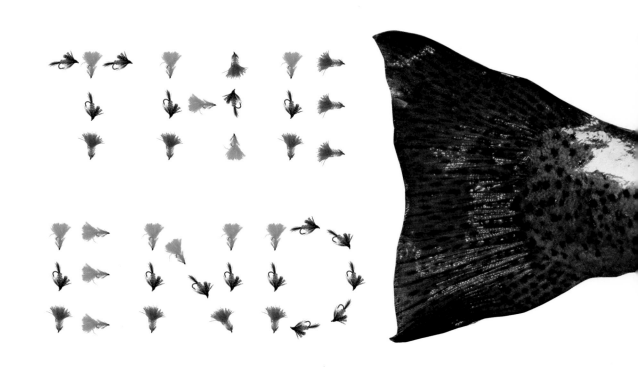

 Royal Wulff

 Black ghost

 Bright Green Attractor (Green Meanie)

 Fall River Special

 Muddler Minnow

 Blue Montana

 Green Stone Fly

 Bead Head Woolly Bugger

 Egg Sucking Leech

 Marabou Leprechaun

 Gray Ghost

Acknowledgements

To Carl Sams and Jean Stoik:
I will be forever grateful that you opened your door and offered encouragement and advice.

To Karen McDiarmid and the team at Precision Color:
Thank you for your pre-press help!

Thank you to my readers and editors along the way:
Linda Whelan and her 2nd graders at Maire,
Treves, Gray, Thad and Cope Lucas, Harry Marvin III + IV, Norm and Jib Harper.

To Grampy: who continues to teach us about flies and knots and casting.

To my three sons and Treves: my team, my inspiration and my joy.

To Trout-tail, the one and only,
may you grow up and continue to do wonderful things!

For more information about this book, go to:

WWW.Trouttail.com

Copyright 2002

ISBN 0-972506-0-3

Printed by Friesens in Canada
Published by Trout-Tail LLC

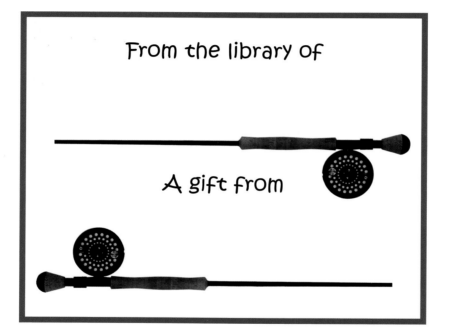

From the library of

A gift from